HACKS
FOR THE NEW
WORLD

**How to Live and Work in the
Age of Sheltering at Home—
and Beyond**

Alyssa Rapp

REDWOOD PUBLISHING, LLC

Redwood Publishing, LLC
Ladera Ranch, California
info@redwooddigitalpublishing.com

Printed in the United States of America

First Printing, 2020

Disclaimer: This book is designed to provide information and motivation to its readers. It is sold with the understanding that the author and publisher are not engaged to render any type of psychological, legal, or any other kind of professional advice. The content of each article is the sole expression and opinion of its author and is not meant to substitute for any advice from your healthcare professionals, lawyers, therapists, business advisors/ partners, or personal connections.

ISBN: 978-1-7344254-6-8 (paperback)
ISBN: 978-1-952106-39-2 (ebook)

Library of Congress Control Number: 2020906729

Cover Design: Michelle Manley
Cover Photo: Robin Subar
Interior Design: Ghislain Viau

First Edition

10 9 8 7 6 5 4 3 2 1

HACKS
FOR THE NEW
WORLD

Dedication

As always, this booklet is dedicated to you, my tremendous husband, Hal Morris, for the daily dose of humor, heavy metal, inspiration, levity, and love that you provide.

It is also dedicated to our Audrey and Henriette, who, in spite of being stuck in the house during these unprecedented times, have maintained a sense of composure and positivity (albeit in between some epic sparring) that impresses me daily.

To my mother, for the ongoing reminder and role modeling that we can get through anything.

For those of you in Surgical Solutions and elsewhere on the front line, I salute and thank you. It's why a portion of the proceeds from the sale of this book will be donated to organizations supporting Covid-19 relief efforts.

Acknowledgments

To Bree Barton, who, once again, provided the editorial prowess to bring this booklet to life.

To Sara Stratton, newest to the Hacks team, thank you for bringing this booklet to life at warp speed!

And to Irina, thank you for the extra kick in the tail to get this done immediately.

Without further ado…

Table of Contents

More Parenting Life Hacks Born Pre-Pandemic But Which Apply in the Shelter-At-Home Era and Beyond

Part 2: 19 Leadership Hacks in the Age of Sheltering-at-Home— and Beyond

Leadership Hack:

A Word from the Author

A reminder for those who've read my first book, *Leadership and Life Hacks: Insights from a Mom, Wife, Entrepreneur, and Executive* (ForbesBooks, October 2019)—and a heads-up for those who haven't—what is a "hack"?

hack *(verb)*
1. cut with rough or heavy blows.
2. an act of computer hacking.

The dictionary defines "hack" as the use of a cutting instrument or a tool for good (hacking off dead branches) or evil (hacking your computer).

For our purposes, I offer an alternate view. Hacks should be thought of as shortcuts, work-arounds, or work-throughs.

You are welcome to read this booklet in any order: in sequence, out of sequence, or just by grabbing the Hack that is relevant to you today. Perhaps tomorrow, you'll find another hack relevant to your parent, sibling, best friend, life partner, business partner, or you again.

No matter how you read this booklet, I'm hoping that one (or many) of the 19 hacks for living and 19 hacks for leading in the age of sheltering at home will prove helpful to you in driving greater efficiency and impact in your life during these unprecedented times—and perhaps even through whatever comes next.

Introduction

When I wrote *Leadership and Life Hacks: Insights from a Mom, Wife, Entrepreneur and Executive* (Forbes-Books, October 2019), I never could have envisioned that less than a year later we would be experiencing a global pandemic. The overall implications of Covid-19 on our world's economic and health systems, short and long term, are still being determined.

Nonetheless, as we all face this new paradigm, we are forced to adapt or, well, adapt. As friends, family, colleagues, and readers have been texting, tweeting, emailing, and WhatsApping me over the past several days and weeks, commenting on how some of the leadership and life hacks have positively impacted them—and inquiring if I had any others—I found myself framing my thoughts and perspective for this strange new world.

While an array of leadership and life hacks from the first book are applicable and poignant in this sheltering-at-home, eLearning-from-home, and working-from-home era, there are also a handful of others that we have developed in our family and business over the past several days and weeks that, I have come to realize, may be helpful to yours.

Hence, the companion edition to *Leadership and Life Hacks* was born.

May the 19 life hacks and 19 leadership hacks in this new and curated *Hacks for the New World: How to Live and Work in the Age of Sheltering at Home—and Beyond* provide you solace, smiles, inspiration, and motivation to push through this period of discomfort—out of this period of "hibernation," to quote my former professor and famed political economist Justin Wolfers, "into the unknown," to quote our daughters' beloved *Frozen 2*, and into the new world on the other side.[1,2]

PART 1

19 LIFE HACKS FOR SHELTERING-AT-HOME

"If you don't like something, change it. If you can't change it, change your attitude."
—Maya Angelou

Life Hacks for Successful E-Learning for School-Age Children and Surviving the Sheltering-at-Home Era

I will leave the creation of curricula to the educational experts and our extraordinary cultural institutions already converting awesome archives of content, leveraging new technologies and creating new relevant digital content. Instead, you'll find below a series of hacks for surviving/managing life with your eager young learners who are now forced to also "work from home," instead of bounding off to school with their friends to learn from experienced and credentialed teachers. Because wow, who knew that working from home while managing children eLearning from home would present such an unprecedented challenge…

I should begin by stating that Hal and I are the proud parents of Audrey Margaret and Henriette Daniella Morris. Audrey is seven and a half, an extrovert, outgoing, impatient, bright, compassionate, dog-loving, sister-jabbing, high-energy, athletic/sports-loving, committed-piano-playing, and stubborn young girl. (Thank you, Husband, for that last one.)

Henriette is five, a dedicated Pre-K student at the French immersion nursery school, and a sweet, mischievous little girl who loves dolls, *Frozen*, LEGOs, ballet, and swimming.

They are opposites in hair color, personality, and style. They are classic sisters: bimodal in their relationship, loving each other/playing beautifully—or fighting like cats and dogs. Calm stasis is the least frequent setting on their shared channel. Hopefully this helps set the stage for the inspiration behind many of the hacks on the following pages.

Life Hack #1

Create new workspaces for your children

Creating new workspaces does not have to mean converting a room in your house into the children's learning center (though that might actually be a good idea if space permits). Creating a designated workspace for your child enables them to think about "going to school" for eLearning in a separate space from where they normally live, eat, and play. This physical separation helped Audrey shift her focus and intention: when she is at her desk, with her Chromebook, workbook, physical books, etc., it is time for "school."

It also helped Henriette start her eLearning from home with her French School pre-K class, which toggles between one-hour sessions on Zoom with the entire class, and one-hour independent work sessions/breaks, three times throughout each day. A desk new to her, with a computer screen new to her, and a new "set-up" for eLearning helped literally and figuratively set the stage for the girls to be "going to school" from home. We even have Henriette continue to put on her school uniform. It's all part of the psychological transition: today is a school day, we go to our desk, it's time to work. With any luck, we'll have planted the seeds for middle schoolers with decent study habits (one can pray).

When the girls take breaks for snacks, lunch, or kinetic wellness (KW), they leave their workspaces for a physical and mental break from their academic subjects.

[P.S. For kinetic wellness—formerly known as physical education or P.E.—we either follow the school's routine of jumping jacks/pushups/sit-ups/etc., or DIY with a 20-minute light treadmill workout, DIY obstacle course inside or outside, or 20-minute outdoor bike ride. Physical movement is crucial to keeping the girls focused, just like it is for adults, needless to say.]

Creating new physical spaces for Audrey and Henriette's eLearning has helped us all set up new routines for success.

Life Hack #2

Set up new routines...
and stick to them

One of my favorite leadership hacks from *Leadership and Life Hacks: Insights from a Mom, Wife, Entrepreneur and Executive* is Life Hack #94: Schedule everything. We have found that this leadership hack applied to home life has helped us in the first weeks of eLearning/sheltering-at-home.

As it relates to our girls, we have found they thrive with standard daily routines more than down-to-the-minute schedules. In these days of eLearning, we've set up new routines. So far, we have kept consistent with some of our "normal" routines already in place: start each day with coloring/stickering/painting/playing in the kitchen while I make breakfast, followed by them getting ready for the day while I work out, followed by a transition to "school."

That transition involves:

(1) Preparing for the day's eLearning activities by printing all required documents for that day, pulling up each required platform or application in the browser so the kid can navigate there with a simple "click," and ensuring all materials required for any non-computer/non-paper assignments (e.g., science experiments, Spanish flashcards, board games) are out and ready to be used that day;

(2) Having the child go to her new dedicated eLearning workspace at roughly the same time each day (8:45 am in our world).

Thankfully, our daughters' elementary/pre-schools have sent tremendous "learning menus" for the weeks of at-home school. These include modules for math, literacy, writing/spelling, science/inquiry, art, and other electives (kinetic wellness, Spanish/French, practicing cursive, etc.). With Audrey, we have made it very clear that selecting four to five of these activities daily, plus 30 minutes of independent reading, is required by their schools and has to be reported back via Google Forms in their daily accomplishments. We have also had success setting up these expectations, then letting the children "choose their own adventure" in terms of which modules to do daily within those broad parameters/requirements.

Wherever possible, we have supplemented science with some of our favorite DIY science activities at home, e.g., *National Geographic* STEM kits, KiwiCrates, and much more for science; an array of awesome board games for ages 5+ to learn addition and subtraction, such as SUM SWAP; and others by Learning Resources. We have had the most fun supplementing their kinetic wellness activities with our own: YogaKids on YouTube, bike rides and scooter rides, running through the fields at the park with Yoda the Bernedoodle, etc.

And speaking of pets, we have added a daily constitutional for Yoda and the girls on their bikes to every school day. It can happen during break one or break two, but getting outside daily—and getting the dog out with the girls—is now part of the new normal. I'm hoping this habit persists long past this sheltering-at-home era.

Life Hack #3

Record (almost) everything your kids do when at-home-schooling

In *Leadership and Life Hacks*, one of the more controversial hacks seemed to be Life Hack #82: If your child throws a tantrum, record it. This is a time-tested tool my husband Hal developed to stymie a tantrum dead in its tracks: he would say nothing, record the tantrum, and play it back for our daughters. Once they saw it, they would stop the behavior immediately. Eventually, their responses became Pavlovian: as soon as Hal would pull out the iPhone to record, they'd stop the tantrum before it even began.

On a far more upbeat note, recording everything in the era of sheltering-at-home/eLearning has positive externalities:

(1) It allows you to readily share your child's at-home learning activities with their teachers (which our elementary school manages through an app called Seesaw, but we manage at home by creating a Google Drive folder per child, per day, and uploading everything she worked on that day to the specific folder—for posterity);

(2) It allows you to record both academic and non-academic progress;

(3) It reminds you of all the creative activities you have done to make it through this "hibernation" phase, which sometimes inspires new activities by jogging the memory of favorites already completed.

Some of our favorite photo or video documentation to date has been: recording the girls' virtual piano lessons, recording their unprofessional but earnest karaoke sessions, recording them painting Daddy's birthday present box instead of using wrapping paper (we were out of adult birthday wrapping paper, and it was a good use of time!), taking a photo of them with their favorite new science experiments (e.g., Why is the ocean salty? Test what happens to an egg in a cup of regular water versus saltwater), and more. For these videos and more, visit AlyssaRapp.com/videos.

Life Hack #4

Pick up a new subject to work on together

loved studying and still love speaking French, and Henriette is in French immersion preschool as a result. But I had not actively participated in her French education until the sheltering in place rules descended upon us as a society. Now, Henriette and I are working on her French vocabulary flash cards, and she, Audrey, and I play French bingo together (where Audrey pulls in her Spanish flashcards so every child is working on her individual language learning). Similarly, Hal is brushing up on his Spanish by joining Audrey for her virtual Spanish education; they work on Spanish vocabulary flash cards and watch YouTube videos conjugating verbs together.

These are the positive benefits. We would likely not have directly invested in this language immersion with our daughters at this level had we not been "forced" to as a result of learning from home. I am hoping these habits will continue post-sheltering in place.

Life Hack #5

Create local "field trips"/DIY art and science experiments

While sheltering-at-home requires us all to hunker down to "flatten the curve," 15-20 minutes of fresh air and sunshine per day are crucial for our health (vitamin D) and sanity. So, provided you are maintaining a safe social distance and observing rigorous hand washing before and after, this can be a great excuse to get outside and learn about one's immediate surroundings. Our daughters have made it a daily ritual to bike ride with Yoda the Bernedoodle as previously discussed; they have also picked some bulbs from our garden to observe how they grow indoors. A weekly favorite includes going to our local beach to pick up rocks to paint, thanks to the recommendation of my cousin Jocelyn Stanton, a star educator who has started her own rock family.[1]

Other friends are planting vegetable seeds in their backyards and labeling them to start vegetable gardens; urbanite friends are even cutting off the tops of green onions and potato eyes and planting them in pots to let them grow on their windowsills.

Any excuse to explore our surroundings with a more attentive eye, appreciate what is around us, and find beauty in the mundane is, well, the perfect way to make lemonade out of lemons in this sheltering-at-home era.

Life Hack #6

Write more letters

One of my favorite assignments our daughter received this week was to write a letter to a family member. Audrey picked her brand-new baby cousin. She shared with him what is happening in her world currently, and asked about his. Best of all, we were able to work on her spelling and grammar through the process (ha).

This week, Audrey had an assignment to write a letter to her new in-class pen pal. She wrote the letter, sharing what eLearning from home has been like for her, then asking what it's been like for him. We then recorded a video of her reading the letter to share with her pen pal in addition to sending the handwritten letter.

In *Leadership and Life Hacks*, I shared Hack #83: Write love letters. In the age of sheltering at home, we've simply adapted this to write more letters, period. Additional ideas could include writing letters to local hospitals to thank the nurses and doctors for their service, or leaving a small Post-It note on your front door for the postal worker, FedEx, or UPS delivery person to say thank you for their ongoing service.

Life Hack #7

Leverage all current art supplies

In the shelter-at-home era, find the beauty in leveraging new DIY art exercises. Not only can you use found objects like rocks for hours of entertainment: it's a perfect opportunity to clear out those half-used art supplies.

We found *Frozen* stenciling kits only partially used, sticker books half done, acrylic paints half used . . . you get the drift. There is no better day than today to use them.

We have even taken it upon ourselves to no longer purchase wrapping paper for friends' gifts. Instead, we use it as an excuse to make our own as we did for Daddy's birthday present. (See below photo and watch a video of how to do this yourself at AlyssaRapp.com/videos.)

Life Hack #8

Revel in the fact that children are adaptable

don't know if I've seen a better example of how adaptable children are than watching Audrey take virtual piano lessons during all of this. At first, it simply seemed like she was practicing. Then when the song finished, with a slight turn of the head to the left, she watched her attentive teacher on FaceTime. He corrected pacing, hand placement, and more. I got choked up watching that moment—not because it was as momentous as other parenting moments, but because of the wonder of how adaptable children are. It gave me faith that the power of technology can bridge us through these strange and uncertain times.

Our piano teachers' ability to teach lessons weekly via FaceTime versus in person is probably the most inspiring adaptation of learning from home I have seen to date. (Watch a video of this at AlyssaRapp.com/videos.)

Life Hack #9

Cook together

We have had a ball making some old favorites together, dressing up other favorites with a new twist, and creating new recipes.

Here are some of the young-child-friendly cooking activities we have enjoyed in the first several weeks of sheltering at home:

- Crepes (new twist: add blueberries!)
  - 1.5 c. milk
  - 1 c. flour
  - 3 eggs
  - (Optional) dash of sugar, dash of vanilla
  - Instructions: Mix all ingredients together, being careful to remove all lumps. Pour 2/3 cup of batter at a time into a hot, greased pan, spreading evenly so thin. When pancake congeals, flip. Put fruit (blueberries!), sugar, etc. (some people like savory things like cheese and meats and vegetables) into the middle, roll, slice, and serve!

- Homemade Pizza
  - Buy premade dough, or follow your favorite pizza dough recipe (usually easy: just flour, water, salt, and sometimes one more ingredient)
  - Knead and roll pizza dough out onto a floured surface

- Spread tomato or spaghetti sauce across pizza dough
- Add your favorite shredded cheeses
- Cook for 12-15 minutes at 400 degrees
- Enjoy!

- Smoothies of all shapes and sizes
  - Milk
  - Yogurt
  - Natural sweetener (raw sugar, honey, jam, etc.)
  - Favorite fruits
  - (Optional) vegan protein powder
  - Ice
  - Instructions: Add to blender, blend, and pour!

- And obviously, no snack hacks would be complete without reprising Life Hack #101 from *Leadership and Life Hacks:* Eat more quinoa.
  - In the sheltering at home era, we continue to have a Tupperware of sprouted quinoa simmered in vegetable broth in our refrigerator at all times. It is the perfect pairing with eggs for breakfast, on salad for lunch, with feta and cherry tomatoes, olive oil, salt, and pepper for a snack, et al.

Life Hack #10

Make music from home

Our new karaoke machine might be the most coveted toy around the house. It creates an opportunity for almost endless hours of self-entertainment as our children find their inner American idols.

There are awesome ways for children to create music while sheltering at home. One website (www.padlet.com) Audrey has explored during this eLearning phase enabled her to use the keyboard/mouse to play a virtual xylophone.[1] Henriette sings her French School song with her class and teachers on Zoom at least weekly.

Whether using wooden spoons on a pot to drum to your favorite song or more high-tech alternatives, there's no better time to find silver lining in this crisis than by making music from home. Even simply singing along to your favorite movie soundtrack on Alexa while playing or cooking can provide a little levity, a little spring in your step, a little extra fun in the sheltering-at-home age. If a spontaneous dance party ensues, all the better…

Life Hack #11

A single smile goes a long,
long way. As does saying THANK YOU

In the rare times that you are interacting at a safe social distance from human beings beyond immediate family members (on a run, when picking up groceries or medicine, etc.), don't forget to smile. A simple smile goes a long, long way. Our Stanford GSB classmate Ron Gutman did a brilliant TED Talk on the hidden power of smiling, which perfectly outlines why smiling matters.[1] In this era of sheltering at home, just try it on for size. It's a small step that can make you and others feel better. Every happy moment counts.

There are equally inspiring examples of cities moved to thank the healthcare providers on the frontlines like London and New York where windows open at 7 pm and a round of city-wide applause takes place in gratitude for the dedication and sacrifice being demonstrated.

And if you have ever felt an inkling to say thank you to someone doing you or your family a service that helps you get through this new way of life, now is the time to say thank you. An extraordinary example of this is a man who puts free hand sanitizer and big 12-packs of toilet paper on his front porch with a sign that said, "Delivery people, please take what you need!"[2]

These are the stories of selflessness, gratitude, and kindness that remind me we are all connected as human beings—and if this can bring out extra goodness, generosity, and gratitude from people's hearts for those on the frontlines, then it would be yet another silver lining from this global pandemic.

Life Hack #12

(Still) do something for yourself DAILY

I n *Leadership and Life Hacks*, I talk about putting on your own oxygen mask first each and every day. In other words, do something to take care of yourself. This holds true as much as ever in the sheltering-at-home age.

Thank goodness for virtual workouts. Whether you are a Peloton devotee (bike/Tread/yoga classes) or can take advantage of your local gym's online offerings, there is an endless array of athletic content to enjoy digitally. My friend and frequent collaborator Bree Barton is offering her weekly "Rock 'n' Write" dance/writing class for free on Zoom.[1] Perhaps this is the time to try something new and get out of your comfort zone—all from the comfort of your own home. All you need is motivation.

The tools exist for your athletic life to stay on track—if not thrive—while sheltering-at-home. Heck, even our daughters have started to look forward to almost daily sessions of YogaKids on YouTube and running at the park or on the treadmill at home. If you weren't already, the sheltering at home era is the PERFECT TIME to start or continue to do something for yourself daily.

And for having made it this far in this booklet, please enjoy one complimentary 60-minute (recorded) coaching session with Abdul Sillah via AlyssaRapp.com/videos. Abdul

Sillah is a trainer to the athletic stars—and a dear personal friend. For years he has coached me, my family, and my team at multiple companies.[2]

Life Hack #13

Schedule virtual coffee chats

had a meeting scheduled with a former colleague right when the crisis hit. Rather than cancel, we kept the meeting as a Google Hangout. Sitting there with our coffee/tea in hand, we had a long-overdue conversation—yes, about the virus and its short-term and long-term economic impact (okay, we're nerds). But also about life *before* sheltering-at-home.

I am setting a goal of at least one virtual catch-up with a friend or colleague each week. FaceTime, Google Hangouts, Zoom: the technology exists. Now the scheduling is just up to you.

That said, set a reasonable limit for how many virtual sessions you commit to daily. One day this week I had a two-hour Google Hangout session followed by a four-hour Zoom Field Leadership team virtual summit. That, simply put, was too much. I now try to keep the sessions to max three hours, and preferably several 45-to-60-minute video sessions in a day with 30-minute breaks to get other work done in between.

Life Hack #14

Schedule virtual cocktail hours

My parents have wildly impressed me with their almost daily FaceTime cocktail hour with friends over the past several weeks. I, too, had a great catch-up via Google Hangouts with a girlfriend I'd been trying to schedule lunch with for weeks. We set the timer at 6pm, our kids were all fed/self-entertaining for that 45-minute timeframe, and we sat, had a glass of wine, and caught up. It wasn't as good as being live, but it was a great substitute given the circumstances. We're planning on round two in a few weeks' time.

In terms of ordering wine online during this pandemic, you are always well served (pardon the pun) to order from wineries directly. They appreciate the support, and many are offering "free shipping included" or other discounts.

Alternatively, some states have now relaxed regulatory requirements to support their local restaurants and ALLOW them to sell not only food for pick-up, but alcohol! These restaurants likely have awesome wines that are well curated and perfectly paired with their menus. If you find your local restaurants are now enabling you to buy food and wine from them, start buying!

Hack #15

Shop local

In this sheltering-at-home era, many local businesses are suffering deeply. In our family, we are doing our best to pre-purchase gift cards, buy meals from local restaurants for pick-up, and do whatever else we can to help buoy their cash flows in these strange and uncertain times.

Some local establishments have already adapted to these changing times and started shipping nationwide as a result of the shelter in place rules. A few of my favorites are below. I hope they inspire you to buy from them and/or from your local retailers:

- Coffee: Who would dare suggest caffeine is not a daily essential? One of our local favorites for coffee and tea: Reprise Coffee Roasters. You can still shop local...by ordering online![1]

- Snacks: Every Body Eat. GF, DF, tasty snacks that everyone in the family will love. Plus you're supporting a start-up cofounded by our GSB classmate Nichole Taylor Wilson.[2] www.everybodyeating.com

- Clothes: Romi's (www.shopromi.com). A stylish yet comfortable curated assortment of clothes, founded by our GSB classmate and friend Romi Mahajan Murphy.[3] See her current offerings on Instagram: https://www.instagram.com/romiboutiquepaloalto/

- Cheese: Cowgirl Creamery[4]
  www.cowgirlcreamery.com

- Fish: Vital Choice Wild Seafood & Organics[5]
  www.vitalchoice.com

- Fruit/Veg: Imperfect Produce.[6] Less expensive than grocery stores, and delivered to your doorstep. www.imperfectfoods.com

- Pre-Packaged Meals: Factor 75[7]
  www.factor75.com

MORE PARENTING LIFE HACKS BORN PRE-PANDEMIC BUT WHICH APPLY IN THE SHELTER-AT-HOME ERA AND BEYOND

Life Hack #16

Nurture your budding entrepreneur

Back in January, before the global pandemic, Audrey received a rainbow loom from dear friends Logan and Christine Derck. The loom was wildly frustrating for the first few days. While I, too, prefer to intuitively build a toy or decode a game, the looming doom of "How do I loom?" proved a ripe opportunity to teach Audrey the next hack...

Life Hack #17

Instructions exist for a reason

Finally, after days of requests, Audrey buckled down and read the instructions. Thereafter, her looming potential was unlocked.

Once she got the hang of it, she was off to the races. Small, colorful rubber-band bracelets were flying off the loom.

After a few days, I came upstairs from working out to a small pile of rainbow-colored, stretchy jewelry. Audrey bounded up to inform me she would be "selling" her bracelets (her idea, not ours!). Those with charms would be $.50, without $.25. She tried to shake me down for a few as I headed for the shower and I informed her that family members who live under our roof would receive the friends-and-family rate of "free" for personal consumption (her gifts to us, if you will). I did have three gifts to buy for others, however, so handed over the $1 (one with charm, two without). We worked on our penmanship when writing receipts. The fledgling loom-based bracelet "business" was born.

Life Hack #18

It's never too soon to teach children the difference between active and passive income. Best case, it inspires them to save

What amused me more is what happened when, in the pre-pandemic era, visitors came to see us over the ensuing weeks. Audrey ran to the door—status quo for our extroverted firstborn—with her looming tool in hand. "Come see the bracelets I've been making!" was her preliminary soft sell. "Which colors would you like for yours?"

And the customization began. "Do you want a charm?"

The shakedown was complete. I interjected at some point in between questions one and two that Audrey was charging for her bracelets, and relayed the pricing. (This was my feeble attempt to instill into our budding entrepreneur Life Hack 18b: It's never too early to learn the importance of truth in advertising.)

And so it went. Bracelets of school colors, favorite football teams, favorite flags, and so on and so forth were born. Customers (house guests) bought. Receipts or thank-you cards were written for "remote" purchases. Piggy the piggy bank started to fill (#Piggypower). Discussions behind the scenes about phase-two lessons to instill about cost of goods sold, marketing via DIY websites vs. Etsy, etc., began to brew.

Just when the "new year, new you" parenting lesson seemed complete, it evolved even further. One Sunday night, before bed, just as this was beginning to rear its ugly head, the girls were with us in our room, and Hal mentioned something about the markets.

Audrey asked, "What is a stock?"

We talked about owning a piece of a company that makes or does things.

"Why should you?" she inquired.

Beleaguered from the day, I decided nonetheless that it was too rich of a teaching moment to pass up, even at eight minutes past bedtime.

"Audrey, do you know how right now you have to make a bracelet or perform a song on the piano at a dinner party to receive a quarter?"

"Or fifty cents!"

"Right, or fifty cents. But you have to make something or do something to get money. That is called 'active' income, as you actively have to do something to earn it.

"But if you saved your quarters and used them to buy shares in a company, that company would go on to make many things—like Peloton bikes or Treads—and every time they sold one, the company would become more valuable.

"Some day, if the company had more money than it needed to invest in its own operations of making bikes or Treads or any other athletic equipment, it would share the profits from the company with its shareholders in the form of dividends. Then you might wake up one day and have made a quarter without having to make a bracelet or play a song."

"Would I get two quarters?"

"If you saved up and bought two shares, you might get two quarters."

[And if you bought an array of stocks, like Peloton, pre-sheltering at home, that deliver content (or services) digitally, you might get those two quarter dividends versus one quarter as soon as the crisis abates...]

Hack #19

Don't reinvent the wheel

Christine Derck relayed that she goes to a handful of Instagram sites for her child gift-giving inspiration (her go-tos are @TheBuyGuide and @TheStrategist).[1]

I personally use the less inventive approach to crowd-sourcing gift ideas for other children: I rinse and repeat the gifts that our kids have received from other kids and loved. Aka, I buy more of them to give other kids! No need to reinvent the wheel when searching for gifts or DIY activities to keep young learners engaged and inspired during their sheltering in place. [E.g., LEGOs, LEGO, LEGOs, and LEGOs are perennial favorites in our home—it seems they are as timeless as wooden blocks.]

PART 2

19 LEADERSHIP HACKS IN THE AGE OF SHELTERING-AT-HOME—AND BEYOND

"Success is not final, failure is not fatal; it is the courage to continue that counts."
–Winston Churchill

There is no question that in a matter of weeks, this virus has brought the US economy to its knees, depleting our healthcare system almost to its core. There is nonetheless a silent army of people across our great country working on the front lines, continuing to fight "The Beast," as the virus is now called by many.

As stated at the top of this book, I greatly appreciate all of the courageous workers at Surgical Solutions and elsewhere on the front lines. It's why a portion of the proceeds from the sale of this book will be donated to organizations supporting Covid-19 relief efforts.

For those not on the front line, a different war has been waged: the daily battle of working from home.

Here is an array of hacks for working from home for team members and leaders alike, hacks that we've developed at Surgical Solutions over the past few weeks as we adapt to having a portion of our team WFH. If any of them are useful to you, hooray!

Leadership Hack #1

Leverage video technology tools for "face-to-face" meetings

It almost goes without saying that the world has replaced physical meetings with digital. But what are best practices for holding team meetings when all are sheltered at home? At the risk of making the implicit explicit: use your favorite video meeting tool—and make people use their cameras!

I love Google Hangouts; my team and the universities at which I teach prefer Zoom; good old FaceTime for 1:1 meetings will also suffice. No matter what, whether meeting face to face or in groups of 2-200, it really, really, really makes a difference for people to TURN ON THEIR CAMERAS.

While there is no substitute for looking people in the whites of their eyes (Leadership Hack #23 in my first book), looking people in the whites of their eyes through a screen is better than nothing. So long as people's cameras are positioned to show them seated at their desks or tables, you can see facial expressions, sense body language, and get a better feel for the interpersonal dynamics when looking at people versus just listening to them. Moreover, it reduces the amount of multitasking that takes place during standard conference calls. This is likely the most important hack for the sheltering in place-coping era of working from home: use video technology in lieu of in-person meetings.

If you are a video meeting super-user, try these bonus video-meeting hacks:

- Zoom: the whiteboard function is pretty slick for toggling between a live discussion and a "brainstorming function."

- Zoom: the backgrounds here bring a little life to Zoom and set the tone of the meeting (e.g., when *don't* palm trees swaying in the background make you smile?).

- Virtual whiteboards in general, e.g., Jamboard by Google.
  - There are several slick whiteboards you can use, Jamboard being a personal favorite. Just be forewarned: your son or daughter might snag your new stylus pens and start mastering the Jamboard app before you do (thank you, Audrey, for decoding it faster than I might have on my own!).

Leadership Hack #2

Schedule everything

Let's call a spade a spade: staying on task while working from home is harder than at an office. There are distractions (e.g., children, dogs, spouses, noises outside your window) and temptations (television on in the background without sound, the snack cupboard being just thirty steps away, etc.).

I've already talked about Life Hack #94 from *Leadership and Life Hacks* in the context of home life. I want to reprise it again here as it relates to work, because it's more valuable than ever as many of us WFH. Schedule every call, every individual deliverable that requires a 15-to-60-minute focused work session—*everything*.

By scheduling external and internal meetings, focused time frames to knock out X deliverable, and even breaks, it is far easier to stay on task than when operating in a sea of distraction.

Leadership Hack #3

Seek episodic versus daily balance for your work life

Seeking episodic versus daily balance (Life Hack #65) might be the most important hack to me personally in *Leadership and Life Hacks*. But I have found that its application to business life is even more relevant when coping with the new shelter in place rules.

This is not a time when we can seek perfect balance, or daily balance, in our work lives. Our frontline healthcare workers are putting in 14-to-20-hour days to address this crisis. For HR teams managing their teams through these crises, it's the same story. My endless gratitude goes out to both of these groups on my own team. I'm sure all other healthcare CEOs would agree.

Furthermore, traditional sales and business development activities have ground to a simmer—if not a halt—while focus is necessarily diverted to pandemic crisis management.

With this lack of time in the case of some, and found time in the case of others, a traditional view of balance (balanced set of activities) in one's work life is not likely to be found. So how can the notion of episodic balance apply?

The shelter at home era can be a time to double down on certain business activities, and all but abandon others, as a mechanism of survival. Balance of business activities can be found on the other side. So what areas of focus can divert an organization's attention in the time of shelter at home? You'll find a few ideas in the leadership hacks below.

Leadership Hack #4

Retool your strategic plan

This is a perfect time to retool strategic plans. Found time can be used to turbo-charge digital lead generation activities; dust off a strategic initiative that had been previously shelved and turn it into a go-to-market plan more quickly than anticipated. It can be a time to explore partnerships that were previously not top-priority, leverage team members capable of X for Y, and so much more. As the adage goes, necessity is the mother of invention. And there is no question that this has created the necessity for most small- and medium-size businesses in America to retool their strategic plans.

Leadership Hack #5

Think and act entrepreneurially

There is no question in my mind that there will be great winners and great losers in businesses as a result of this. The tourism industry will take a long time to rebound. Medical supply companies stand to be big winners, as do on-demand athletic companies like Peloton and ecommerce giants like Amazon. And there are countless in between.

It is also no secret that entrepreneurs are capable of adapting with lightning speed, pivoting strategies as needed, and frankly doing whatever it takes to survive.

For this reason, what's happening might provide the greatest opportunity for economic disruption to start-ups across America, greater than they have ever seen—and greater than they might ever see again. As businesses are essentially forced to stop their races dead in their tracks, everyone will have to return to the starting blocks post pandemic.

With this unanticipated global economic reset, the fastest, speediest, and hungriest to win have the fastest starts out of the starting blocks. To quote Abdul Sillah, while it is not how you start a race but how you finish it that determines greatness, those start-ups that are nimble, agile, and speedy will have an unprecedented opportunity to get going and get going quickly—provided their unique solution to a problem is relevant and vital during the age of Covid-19. They will certainly have an opportunity to battle the greats faster and more furiously than they would have otherwise.

So if you are an established organization, it's time to think entrepreneurially in order to stay afloat and thrive during and post this new era. And if you are an entrepreneur: lace up, prepare, and get ready to fly. This could be your time.

Leadership Hack #6

Use the crisis as an excuse for forming new habits/a new type of team bonding

I agree with Rahm Emanuel: "Never allow a good crisis go to waste. It's an opportunity to do the things you once thought were impossible." With this in mind, I tapped Abdul Sillah to create a daily workout for my team in the name of Surgical Solutions' "100 Days of Healthy" in the shelter-at-home era. I hope the crisis subsides while the 100 Days persists. Why do this now, in this era? Because there is "no day but today," to quote my brother Anthony Rapp's prescient words in RENT.

Leadership Hack #7

Let's use this crisis as an impetus
to make material investments
in our nation's ability to fight
the next public health crisis

Rahm expounds upon his recommendation to "never allow a good crisis to go to waste" in a recent article in the Washington Post.[1] In it, he makes several points that are relevant leadership hacks in the era of sheltering-at-home. The most poignant point IMHO is, "Let's finally make the investment in public health that's been so lacking. To get ahead of the next pandemic, we need to invest not only in the CDC and the Food and Drug Administration but also the National Institutes of Health, which funds the research behind new medicines and vaccines." So let's do it.

Leadership Hack #8

Search for potential new strategic opportunities as a result of the crisis

have been wowed by demonstrations of innovation during the pandemic: Bloom Energy adapting its capabilities to repair broken ventilators; Tesla partnering with Medtronic to produce more ventilators; the primary manufacturer of testing swabs in Maine ramping up for mass production seemingly overnight.

We at Surgical Solutions are looking for opportunities to support pop-up hospitals during the Covid-19 crisis and to leverage our team to provide additional support for our current hospital partners as they request it, or as we anticipate it. Adaptation seems to be the name of the game here, and where one can adapt, new value can often be created.

Leadership Hack #9

Overcommunicate versus undercommunicate with your people before, during, and after a crisis

As the days of the pandemic commenced, I sensed natural fears in our team out in the field. Would their hospitals be impacted to the degree of those in New York City? Would their elective surgeries be cancelled, as had the surgeries at many of the coastal hospitals they'd seen on TV?

We have very good habits and cadence for communicating with our senior leadership team, our field leadership team, and our team as a whole through email, Slack, and as of January 2020, Town Halls.

Those of you who read my first book know I'm a firm believer in the value of overcommunicating versus undercommunicating (Leadership Hack #42), and this is never truer than in a time of crisis. Hence why we stepped up our game during the days and weeks leading up to the peak of it:

- HR sent weekly (if not more frequent) companywide emails on the fast-changing federal regulations that would impact (benefit) worker forces like that of Surgical Solutions;

- I personally conducted weekly 30-minute Town Halls open to the entire company for the three weeks in March leading up to the introduction of Federal

Benefits (April 1, 2020) to elucidate our strategies and answer any live questions from our team in the field;

- We created a new Slack channel on Covid-19 and encouraged ongoing questions and answers from the team that all could see.

I believe that transparency and timeliness instill confidence, even if the news isn't ideal. For this reason, I addressed the team live, shared how we were planning to navigate through these choppy waters, and why our business strategy and purpose would be just as valued on the other side of this, if not more so.

The responses I received buoyed me. "You were meant for this type of leadership," one team member wrote. "I cannot thank you enough for having the courage to tell it to us straight, even if the truth isn't ideal," wrote another. There is no question in my mind that this was the right approach—and I have every expectation of continuing to overcommunicate versus undercommunicate through the same channels as we eventually pull out of this crisis, perhaps becoming even busier than we were before.

Leadership Hack #10

Thank your customers

Last year we started a simple, bimonthly email communication strategy with current and prospective customers, a "nurture" campaign in marketing speak.

In the first weeks of the crisis, we sent one email to this list from me personally, with a simple message of "Thank you for all you are doing." It was the most opened campaign we have sent to date. It was also the most forwarded campaign. Some even responded to my email directly, thanking me for thanking them.

Surgical Solutions is far from alone in this practice. There have been an abundance of clever marketers in this sheltering-at-home era, everyone from airlines to restaurants to wineries, offering endless specials, discounts, 20-percent-off deals—anything to keep their brands top-of-mind for their customers while providing them with something of unique value in these strange times. That said, a few have gone overboard, almost like a desperate political candidate's email campaign—you know it when you see it. Your customer relationships must be bespoke. Offering up digital classes when you were normally an analog yoga studio? Great thing to do and announce weekly. Just remember that less is more, and authenticity always wins.

Leadership Hack #11

Turn any physical value proposition digital that you can

The very best examples of this are our nation's great cultural institutions. American Ballet Theater released some of its archival video footage online. The National Archives Museum and countless other museums send emails with enriching content and actionable, printable related activities. Most of higher education—as well as K-12—is turning to virtual classrooms for the entire spring quarter. And as we've discussed, yoga studios and health, wellness, and fitness centers are providing digital content to their members.

Bottom line: if there is something you typically do in person but can offer up during this time virtually? Do it. Voice lessons? Ballet class? My favorite so far was a truffle risotto demonstration. No reason you as a business cannot leverage your unique talents in this digital age—you just need to leverage creativity and technology to do so.

Leadership Hack #12

Load up on great background music

On a far lighter note, and in the spirit of "celebrating good times" (see Chapter 9 in *Leadership and Life Hacks* for all the good party tricks), there is no reason NOT to jam to your favorite tunes while working from home—unless music will disrupt your meeting or distract you while cranking out a project. Otherwise, the beauty of working from home is that it allows you those slight creature comforts you don't get at an office, e.g., working on your favorite chair or couch, in your robe, with your favorite mug, with your favorite tunes in the background. What's not to like?

Leadership Hack #13

Acknowledge fear of the pandemic and move through it

The crisis had an unprecedented beginning—and has an unknown end. Anything this nebulous naturally produces fear. Fear gets a bad rap, but it's there for a reason: to protect you from something. Just like standing on a balance beam is scary because your life and limbs are at risk, so too is making a business decision like to pivot versus quit, which carries huge risk. This is another hack (Leadership Hack #9) from my first book that I'm dusting off and reusing here, because as we all know, fear is running rampant right now. It's hard to wean off the constant news drip of uncertainty and dire predictions. Fear is a normal human response. The trick is in not letting it dominate your psyche.

Allow yourself your daily dose of fear, but then move through it. I realize we all want to stay informed, and that's important as expectations and the correct course of action regarding Covid-19 are rapidly changing. That said, being paralyzed by fear is never to anyone's advantage, not pre-, intra-, or post-Covid-19. As always, your job is to acknowledge the fear—to take note of its presence—and then push through it.

Leadership Hack #14

All great ideas start with "What if?"
Never be afraid to ask "What if?" over
and over, until you find a solution

Much of the best entrepreneurial innovation in the U.S. over the past twenty years has come from Silicon Valley, precisely because of the constant willingness to ask and re-ask, "What if?"

Some people's response to challenges or obstacles is to stop asking questions. If you want to solve a problem, you have to open yourself up to the possibility that change is inevitable, and reframing the problem will present an otherwise undiscovered solution. My favorite question to ask myself as an entrepreneur and executive—a question I even ask my students—is, "If not this, what, and if not now, when?"

A prime example of this came recently while speaking to a local entrepreneur with a side hustle/passion for cooking healthy Asian cuisine. She has a nutrition degree, a chef license, and had never made a go of it as a private chef or catering business. So I said to her, "While your primary business (nail salons) is closed due to Covid-19, why not test if you could start a home catering business with 8 to 10 families, delivering them each 3 to 4 meals a week, during Covid-19 only?" If it worked, perhaps she'd find the seedlings for her next enterprise. It's a perfect, low-risk, high-potential reward timeframe to test her next entrepreneurial idea.

In short, there is no better time to apply the "What If?" approach to problem solving.

Leadership Hack #15

If you want other people to follow you off the ledge, you better be ready to lead by example

If you want your team to be all in, they have to see that you're all in first. You have to acknowledge the unprecedented circumstances, yet retain a clarity of purpose and clarity of vision that will inspire everyone to tack the boat for a new island, and row like hell to get there.

These pandemic seas are choppy. For all of us. But if you're asking your team to hang on, then you better see an island to which you're paddling, commit to it yourself, and not quit until you lead your team there.

Leadership Hack #16

Make sure your team is fully aligned around the same goal, on a specific timeline, so that everyone is sprinting, before, during, and after the Covid-19 era

From where we currently sit, it is not 100 percent clear when "normalcy" will return. But ensuring that everyone on your team is on the same page as to what the goal is *today* (survival) and the corporation's goal and purpose on the other side of this crisis is crucial.

Then, set a realistic expectation as to the timeline required to withstand the current circumstances. I know that seems counterintuitive given that no one knows when we will have reached the "peak" of the curve—or when it will be flattened back to pre-Covid-19 times. That said, we at Surgical Solutions suggested that we expected things to be really, really challenging for 30 days (April 2020), then we would re-evaluate and extend our timeline by 15-45 days, as needed. Most of us can get through 10 seconds, 10 days, even 10 weeks of almost anything—if we know it will have an end. It's just an exercise in psychological discipline to withstand the discomfort and make it through.

Leadership Hack #17

Be generous

The global pandemic has spared seemingly few nations, and you'd be hard pressed to find anyone who has not been either directly or indirectly affected. Small acts of kindness, of generosity, go a long way. Generosity can start right at home—and right within your company. See a terrific co-worker go out of his or her way for another? Send a $25 iTunes gift card in thanks. Realize you have too many meals coming to your house one week? Divert one to another team member just because. See your children's artwork piling up around your house? Pop it in the mail to a colleague who may need a smile. Have a team member celebrating his/her birthday at home? Send flowers to make them feel special albeit self-isolated. There is almost zero downside to individual generosity—and small acts of brightness are never more valuable than today.

Leadership Hack #18

Read more books

Self-serving as it sounds, I have a stack of business books by my bedside table, and I am committed to getting through one every two weeks during my sheltering at home. There is no better time to review great lessons learned by business leaders around the globe and sharpen your intellectual sword for battle on the other side of this pandemic.

Leadership Hack #19

Share best practices

We are all developing tools for leadership and management in this new shelter-at-home era. My goal in *Hacks for the New World* has been to share thirty-eight of these tools with you. I encourage you to share the tools and "hacks" you have developed, too, to the degree that you feel comfortable—perhaps via class listservs with fellow alumni, in other business or entrepreneurial groups you're a part of, via phone with competitors who are friendly foe, or via email with your customers.

There is no question that we are all in this together. The more you are able and willing to share your learnings, if for no other reason than to help another player through these unprecedented times, you will feel good for having done so. Even better: you will have potentially helped another business leader along the way. And you never know when you'll need those karma chips down the road. Share a surgical mask today: get a surgical mask tomorrow.

Conclusion

These are strange times. I toggle between days of gratitude for the new normal—more time with my husband and our children, conquering hours of digital meetings somehow productively, squeezing in a double workout—and days of pure frustration, juggling printer jams for children's weekly eLearning in concert with urgent morning Zoom sessions in tandem with Hal's iPhone dying unceremoniously and needing to be replaced by our back-up in the midst of the children's lessons/that emergency work call.

It's a rollercoaster ride—like so much of life. The best lesson I have learned on any rollercoaster ride is to buckle up and try to take the peaks and valleys in stride. Celebrate the wins with arms held high, and breathe through the lows. So long as the coaster stays on the track, you are winning.

Success during a pandemic in my mind is defined by attitude and effort. Did I give a certain activity my all? Did I give a certain obligation my all? Or did I realize it wasn't crucial and then choose to leave it on the field? If the answer is yes, then, to quote my great husband Hal, effort is all you can control. There will be Zoom video bombers and printer jams. There will be barking dogs in the background of important work calls and employee stressors previously unimagined. Staying positive—and working hard, each day, every day—are two things within my control. In the time of crisis, as always, until it's the 9th inning, and the last out: one must keep swinging.

As for the rollercoaster? To the degree that you can find ways to enjoy the ride, summon valor in the journey, discover small tokens of gratitude for the little gifts life is bringing in spite of the madness, and celebrate those small wins—then my wish for you is that those bright lights can buoy you on this winding journey as much as they have for me.

If *Hacks for the New World: How to Live and Work in the Age of Sheltering at Home—and Beyond* serves as one of those small sources of inspiration for you, I have abundant gratitude—and would love to hear from you.

Twitter @alyssarapp
Instagram: @alyssajrapp
Facebook: @alyssarapp
Web: **www.alyssarapp.com**

Additional Books by Alyssa Rapp

amazon.com/author/alyssarapp

Leadership and Life Hacks: Insights from a Mom, Wife, Entrepreneur and Executive, published by ForbesBooks in October 2019.

Bottlenotes Guide to Wine: Around the World in 80 Sips, published by Adams Media in October 2008.

Resources & Links

General:

To access the videos mentioned throughout as well as additional videos showing more hacks in action, please visit: AlyssaRapp. com/videos.

Introduction:

1. https://twitter.com/JustinWolfers
2. https://movies.disney.com/frozen-2

Life Hacks:

Life Hack #5: Create local "field trips"/DIY art and science experiments

   1. https://www.instagram.com/rockbyrock/

Life Hack #10: Make music from home

   1. www.padlet.com

Life Hack #11: A Single Smile Goes a Long, long way. As does saying THANK YOU

1. https://www.ted.com/talks/ron_gutman_the_ hidden_power_of_smiling?language=en
2. https://www.tiktok.com/@evaneramagic/ video/6806362411231202566

Life Hack #12: (Still) do something for yourself DAILY

1. https://www.instagram.com/speakbreely/
2. https://www.instagram.com/AbdulSillah1/

Life Hack #15: Shop Local

1. https://www.repriseroasters.com/
   - https://www.repriseroasters.com/store
2. www.everybodyeating.com
3. www.shopromi.com
   - https://www.instagram.com/ romiboutiquepaloalto
4. www.cowgirlcreamery.com
5. www. vitalchoice.com
6. www.imperfectfoods. com
7. www.factor75.com

Life Hack #19: Don't Reinvent the Wheel

1. https://www.instagram.com/TheBuyGuide/
2. https://www.instagram.com/TheStrategist/

Leadership Hacks:

Leadership Hack #7: Let's use this crisis as an impetus to make material investments in our nation's ability to fight the next public health crisis

1. Emanuel, Rahm. "Opinion | Let's Make Sure This Crisis Doesn't Go to Waste." The Washington Post. WP Company, March 25, 2020. https://www.washingtonpost.com/opinions/2020/03/25/lets-make-sure-this-crisis-doesnt-go-waste.

Made in the USA
Monee, IL
10 July 2020